Crayon Art

This edition published in 2016
By SpiceBox™
12171 Horseshoe Way
Richmond, BC
Canada V7A 4V4

First published in 2015
Copyright © SpiceBox™ 2015
Text and photographs copyright © Parramón Ediciones, S.A. 2007

ISBN 10: 1-77132-234-9
ISBN 13: 978-1-77132-234-8

CEO & Publisher: Ben Lotfi
Editorial: Ania Jaraczewski
Creative Director: Garett Chan
Art Director: Christine Covert
Design & Layout: Charmaine Muzyka
Production: James Badger, Mell D'Clute
Sourcing: Janny Lam, May Ko

For more SpiceBox products and information,
visit our website: www.spiceboxbooks.com

Manufactured in China

3 5 7 9 10 8 6 4

Contents

Introduction to Crayons

You've probably used wax crayons for lots of art projects at home and at school. Crayons are great when you start to draw and paint because they're so easy to use. They're soft enough that you can color large areas quickly, and you can color in lots of different ways, as you will learn in this book.

Crayons are usually sold in boxes in lots of bright colors. It's also easy to mix colors, which means you can draw in pretty much any color you want! Crayons are soft because they contain an oily or waxy material, usually paraffin wax. They can be used to paint on almost any surface, so play around and have fun coloring!

Tools & Materials

Crayons usually come in a box of different colors. When they're new they have a nice, pointy tip, but since crayons are soft this point usually gets worn down quite quickly.

Making art with crayons is more like painting than drawing. Because they're soft and oily, it's easier to paint using broad strokes than it is to draw thin lines with lots of detail, although you can do both.

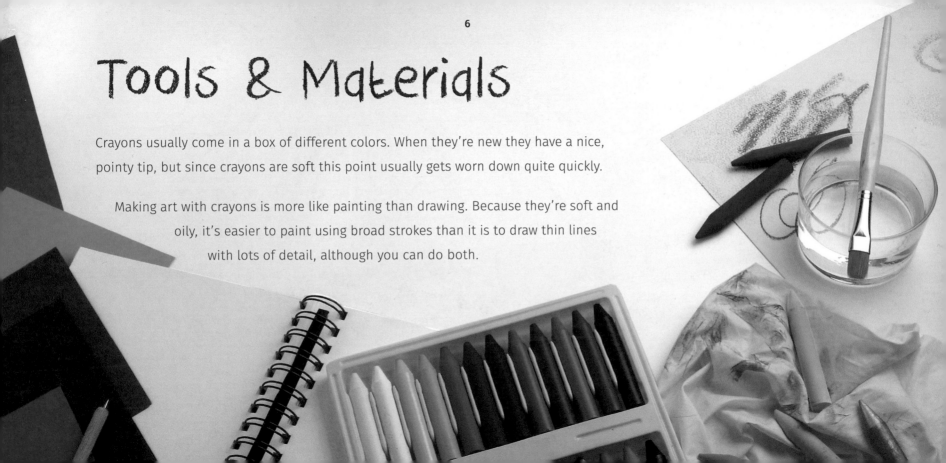

If you're starting off with a sketch done in pencil, make sure you draw large shapes and open spaces instead of lots of little details. Then you can use your crayons with broad, sweeping strokes.

There are two types of wax crayons. The most common is an oily, wax-based crayon which is the type you use at school. It's very soft and is great for painting. There's also a kind of watercolor crayon that is a bit harder, which makes it easier to draw details. You color with it as usual, but when you brush over it with water it dissolves and creates a pretty watercolor effect.

You might think that there are not many ways to use crayons, but you can actually create a lot of really interesting effects with different tools. Let's take a look at some of the different things you can do with crayons.

The most useful tool that you can use is your own two hands, especially your fingers! You can decide for yourself which hand and which fingers are the most comfortable to work with. If the painting is quite big you may even want to use the side of your hand.

Remember that dirty fingers and hands will stain the paper, so it's important to always wipe your hands clean between each color you use. Also, keep in mind that your skin contains oils, which can help to soften and blend the crayons as you work.

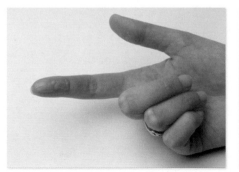

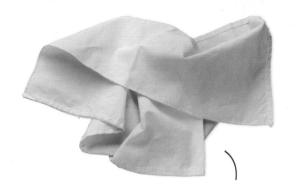

You will see in later exercises that there is a fun technique called **scratching**. To do this, you can use a stylus or anything that has a pointed tip but isn't too sharp, like a toothpick, the cap of a pen or the handle of a paintbrush.

If you want to erase color, and not just smudge or blend it, try using a rag or cotton balls. They don't contain any oils, so you'll be able to remove color better than by wiping with your finger.

Paintbrush handle

Lid from a ballpoint pen

Toothpick

Crayon can also be removed using a spatula, palette knife or any other tool that has a flat edge that you can use to gently scrape the color off with.

Crayons & Color

Primary Colors

Red, yellow and blue are called **primary colors** because they are not made up of any other colors, but you can mix them to get lots of new colors.

Secondary Colors

Secondary colors are made by mixing two primary colors together. If you mix red and yellow you get orange. Combining yellow and blue will give you green. Blue mixed with red will become purple.

Complementary Colors

If you take a primary color and put it next to a secondary color that's made up of the other two primary colors mixed together, you get a pair of **complementary colors**. Red is complementary to green. Yellow is complementary to purple. Blue is complementary to orange. These colors will look lively beside each other in your art.

Color Wheel

The **color wheel** shows how all the colors
are related to each other. The biggest circles
are the primary colors. See how they make a
triangle? In between the primary colors are the
secondary colors, which are the next biggest
circles. Each secondary color sits between the
two primary colors that are combined to make
it. The smallest circles are mixed colors like
yellow-orange and blue-green.

You can see how complementary colors are
always opposite each other on the color wheel.

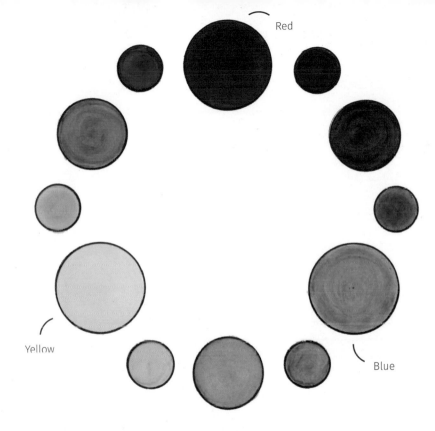

Red

Yellow

Blue

A Few Tips

Now that you know a little more about crayons, it's the time to start painting! Remember these tips, as they will be a big help in your work.

The first thing is to prepare the table or surface where you'll be painting. Cover it with a few layers of newspaper to protect it, since crayons can be a bit messy!

Keep your crayons organized in their box, instead of just loosely thrown together.

Clean the tip of the crayon with a paper or cloth every time you use it.

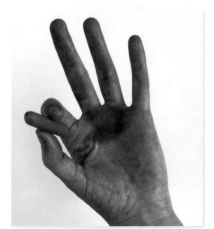

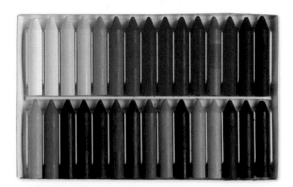

Crayon is hard to erase. If you need to fix a mistake, try to scrape off as much of the crayon as possible with a metal spatula, then paint over it with a white crayon. Finally, add the color that you wanted to paint with over top. The best idea, though, is to make a plan of what you're going to do before you start, so you don't need to erase your work very often.

Crayons can be used to draw lines or to color. The line may be fine—drawn with only the tip—or thick, using the side of the crayon. You might find it helps to break the crayon into smaller pieces so you can color more easily.

Finally, if you want to protect your work from heat or accidental scrapes, cover your painting with a fixative or a spray varnish.

Blending Colors

As you've seen, there are many colors of crayons, and you can get interesting effects by mixing colors together. But how do you blend colors? There are two techniques you can use: cold and warm.

Cold Technique

With this technique, you first paint with one color, and then pick another color to paint over top of the first. The second color you use needs to be a bit more see-through than the first color. These transparent colors—like yellow, orange and green—are the ones you would paint over the more opaque colors like brown and blue.

A mix with white

A mix of two crayon colors

Materials: crayons and drawing paper

1. Draw a lollipop on a stick and paint it yellow.

2. Draw a few lines in blue on the right side of the lollipop.

3. Color in a red area at the bottom left of the lollipop, and you have finished your three-flavored candy. Yummy!

The white crayon is special. Although it is fairly opaque, it can be used to paint over other colors. Try coloring with it and you will see that when you mix it with another color, the first color becomes lighter, and you also get some very pretty results.

Warm Technique

When you mix crayons using the warm technique, the order in which you apply the colors doesn't matter. Wax melts with heat, so after you color the area, use your finger to rub the colors together. The heat from your finger will soften the colors and help to blend them together.

If you mix complementary colors, you will darken the color and turn it grayish. If you want your colors to stay bright and fresh, use colors that are in the same part of the color wheel, like yellow and red, or green and blue.

1. Draw a lollipop and color it red.

2. Add a large white area to show where the light is hitting it.

3. Use a circular motion with your finger to warm the wax and blend the colors together.

Monochrome

For this exercise, pick out a color that you like. For our example we chose red. Think about all the different reds you know of: carmine, scarlet, raspberry, poppy, cherry, coral, strawberry, faded red, lobster, pepper, tomato, light red, wine and so on.

Now it's time to discover how you can make an endless number of reds or whatever color you have chosen. It helps to understand values and tones of colors, so let's look at what these words mean.

Value describes how light or dark a color is, meaning how much black or white it contains. If you add black to the red, a little at a time, it will get darker and darker until it is almost black. Or, if you add white to the red, you will see that it gets lighter and lighter, until it is a very pale pinkish-white color.

You can also add a little bit of other colors to the color you picked. For example if you start with the same red color and add a bit of yellow to it, you will get an orangeish-red. If you mix it with blue, you will get maroons and purples.

Now that you know how to make different tones and values of a color, try to make a monochrome painting with crayons!

Warm & cool colors

Materials: crayons, drawing paper and a pencil

Think about cold things...and now think about hot things. When you were thinking about ice and cold weather, did you imagine tones of blues, grays and greens? And when you thought about hot, spicy food and sunny days, did you think about yellows, reds and oranges? That's what we mean when we talk about color temperature.

In a color wheel, the **cool colors** and the **warm colors** are opposite each other. Look at the color wheel on page 11 and see if you can figure out which ones are the warm colors and which are the cool colors.

Experiment to see what happens when you mix a cool color with a warm color. If you mix a blue with a yellow, you'll get green. If you are mixing red and blue you will get violet. But if you mix orange with green, what color will you get?

If you look at the color wheel you will see that the colors opposite each other on the circle are complementary. When you mix these colors together they make some very dark, dull colors. On the other hand, colors that are sitting near each other on the color wheel will create nice bright colors when mixed.

Mixing green and orange

Mixing blue and red

Mixing blue and yellow

1. Imagine a drawing that has a cold area and a warm area. Make a light sketch with a pencil.

2. Start to add color, beginning at the top and working your way down. This will help you keep from smudging your work.

3. Mix warm and cool colors to make new colors in your drawing, so that your painting will be more interesting and lively.

In this picture, the sun and the boat at the top of the page are done in warm tones, and the ocean is done in cool tones. We finished with more warm tones at the bottom of the ocean.

Textures

Materials: crayons and drawing paper

Every object around us has its own **texture**. With crayons you can make it look like the things you draw have realistic textures, and create some very interesting effects in your work.

Sun - Over a yellow background, draw circular lines with an orange crayon, but don't press too hard. Then do the same thing with a yellow crayon, which will blend into the orange.

Towel - To make a fabric texture, color the whole towel with one color, and then make the horizontal and vertical lines using the very tip of two different colored crayons.

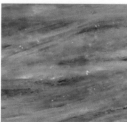

Ocean - Draw lots of horizontal lines with navy blue, light blue, dark green and light green to make the waves. Then blend the lines with a white crayon by making wavy lines over top.

Sky - Remove the paper label from a sky-blue crayon, and color in the sky using the side of the crayon. Fill the entire area of the paper, except the area for the white cloud.

Cloud – In the space that you left white, make circular strokes with a white crayon to create a fluffy cloud. Overlap it with the blue sky a bit, mixing the blue color into the white cloud.

Umbrella – Color the umbrella pole gray, and the umbrella panels with red, orange and yellow. Then use a white crayon to draw lines in between each of the panels to separate them.

Sand – Remove the paper label from a light brown crayon and very lightly fill in the sand area, coloring with the crayon on its side. With dark brown, make small lines and dots to give the sand texture.

volume

Materials: crayons, drawing paper and a pencil

Creating a look of **volume** will help you make a picture that seems three dimensional, even though you are drawing on a flat surface. To do this, you will have to show where the light is coming from by drawing highlights and shadows.

There are different ways of showing shadows: you can add a bit of black or dark blue to the area in shade, or you can mix the color with its complement.

Draw three objects with a simple, three-dimensional shape. It could be a ball or a box, but here we have drawn three cylinders that are going to become lanterns. Color each one a primary color.

Remember that the complementary color of yellow is purple, the complement of blue is orange, and the complement of red is green.

To give a sense of volume you have to paint the shadow on each lantern. Figure out where the light is coming from. The area opposite the light source is where the shadows fall. Color these areas with the complementary color of the lantern.

All colors have a complement, not just the primary colors. If you look at the color wheel you will see that complementary colors sit directly opposite each other. Now try making shadows using complementary colors with other colors on the wheel.

Crayons on Wood

Materials: piece of wood, wax crayons, liquid watercolors and a pointy tool like a stylus

Wood is a great surface for coloring on with crayons. Besides painting and blending the colors, you can also etch on the colored areas.

In this example, we will make use of the waxy texture of the crayons to experiment with painting watercolors over top.

1. Draw an African mask design on a piece of thin plywood. Then draw a border all around the edge.

2. Color the mask and frame with crayons. Use regular wax crayons for this project.

3. To add more details, use a pointy tool to scratch marks into the colored areas. You can make triangles, semicircles, etc.

4. Now paint the background of your mask picture with watercolors. When you brush over the parts colored with crayons, the paint will not stick to the wax.

5. To finish, you can color the border with patterns and shapes. You may need to erase the pencil lines a bit first if you are using light-colored crayons, or the lines will show through.

It's a good idea to finish your work with a wood varnish, because it will set the colors and protect them from fading or being damaged.

Drawing Surfaces

Materials: crayons, corrugated cardboard, compass tool, tracing paper, coarse sandpaper, card stock, sandpaper, acetate, aluminum foil, cork, drawing paper, scrap fabric, scissors and glue

Why don't we draw the solar system? Look for photos of the planets in a book or on the Internet. Notice how each one seems to have a different surface. You'll see that changing the type of material you color on will create many different effects.

Before you start making the textures, color a piece of thick cardboard a deep blue for the outer-space background. Draw a circle in a different size on each of the surfaces you've collected.

Uranus - Tracing paper is perfect for using blending techniques to create a smooth texture.

Mercury - Paint with a gray crayon over a piece of card stock.

Jupiter - Crayons only stick to the very top of the surface of sandpaper, giving a rough texture.

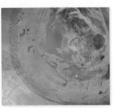

Pluto - Draw Pluto on acetate (clear plastic) and lay part of it over another planet, which will show underneath.

Saturn - It's difficult to color evenly and uniformly on aluminum foil, but the results are very interesting.

Mars - Paint a circle of cork with different tones of red and then blend the colors with your finger.

Neptune - Use a piece of scrap fabric. Crayon will make the texture of the fabric more visible.

Venus - Paint over a piece of cardboard, then cover it with white wax to make the texture of the cardboard stand out.

Earth - Crumple up a piece of paper and then flatten it again. Color over it with the sides of a brown and a blue crayon and see how the colors mark up the wrinkles.

Now glue the planets onto your space background, and you have your own solar system!

Reserves

Materials: crayons, card stock, drawing paper, scissors, tape and round stickers

In this exercise, you will be using reserves and templates to create shapes with your crayons.

A **reserve** lets you leave an area of the paper blank. Here you will use a template to cover the area and create an outline to follow. With this technique, you don't have to be too worried about making a detailed sketch, and you can experiment with different effects.

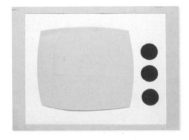

1. Cut out four strips of thick paper and stick them to your drawing surface in the shape of a rectangle. Next cut out a square with rounded sides and stick it into the middle of the rectangle where the screen would be. Then, with round stickers, make three more reserves for the buttons.

2. Once all of the templates are in place, color the space around the screen with strong strokes, but make sure you don't move the templates.

3. Without removing the templates, use dark blue to make an outline around the TV, the screen and the buttons.

4. Now remove all of the templates carefully, and you will see that you have the shape of a TV.

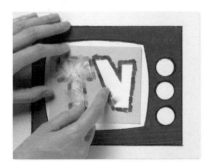

5. Cut the letters "TV" out of a piece of card stock so that you can use the paper outline, not the letters themselves. Then pick out some colors and paint the letters inside the template. Use your finger to smudge the colors toward the middles of the letters.

6. To make the antennae, cut out a template as you did for the letters, and color it in. For a nice finish, you can use the point of a pair of scissors to scrape lines into the border of the TV, or decorate around the buttons.

Grattage

Materials: crayons, card stock, and a stylus or other pointy tool

Grattage is a painting technique that works especially well with crayons. It's when you make different layers of color and then scrape some of the top layer away with a pointy tool so that you can see the colors underneath. First let's look at how to pick colors that work well for this technique. Then you will be ready to put what you know into practice.

Paint an area yellow and then cover it with dark green. Now make some small scratches in the green and you will be able to see the yellow, right? This combination works because the green is much darker than the yellow.

Try again with a dark blue mark, and then cover it with orange. Scratch a design into the orange, and you will notice that you can hardly see the design. That is because the orange isn't strong enough to cover such a dark color.

Finally, make an orange mark, then cover it with red and scratch in your design. You can see the orange design in the red, but barely, because the two colors are so similar that there is not a lot of contrast between them.

1. Make a drawing with a pencil and start coloring it with light crayon colors: yellow, sky blue, light green, orange and so on.

2. Once you have painted the first layer, add a second layer of color over the areas where you want to scratch your design. The top layer should be darker than the first layer.

3. Now all you have to do is scratch out an interesting design using a stylus or some other pointy tool!

You can create the same effect using colored paper, and painting one layer of color over top. Once you scratch in your design, you will see the color of the paper coming through.

Watercolor Crayons

Materials: watercolor crayons, watercolor paper, masking tape, paintbrush and a pencil

Watercolor crayons are exactly like the regular crayons you use for coloring, but they are specially designed so that they can be blended with water. This means you can use them both as regular crayons and watercolors at the same time! Let's give it a try. Choose a color and start coloring a picture. Then dip a paintbrush in water and paint over the color. The crayon color turns into transparent watercolor.

Tip: The crayons in your kit will create a nice watercolor effect.

1. Before you can work in this medium, you need to stretch your paper on a drawing board. To do this, just tape all the edges of the paper to a drawing board or to the table.

2. Make a drawing with your pencil. In this example, we've drawn a circus.

3. Color the sky, the grass and the trees with the watercolor crayons.

4. Get your paintbrush wet and brush it over the watercolor crayon.

5. Now create a palette of watercolors. To do this, color with your watercolor crayons on a separate piece of paper, and when you want to paint with them, dampen the colors with a wet brush and pick up the color to use in your picture.

6. The final details can be drawn in with the crayons, without getting them damp.

Crayons on Acetate

Materials: watercolor crayons, watercolor paper, masking tape, paintbrush and a pencil

Let's have some fun drawing on a sheet of acetate, or clear plastic.

There are lots of things you can do with acetate—use your imagination!

Give it a try!

To start, you'll need to do a sketch in pencil on a piece of paper, and then place the acetate over the sketch and trace over it with your crayons.

The nice part about using acetate is that you can leave some parts uncolored, and put colored papers or textures underneath which will show through the picture. Just change the background paper to change the look of your picture!

1. On a piece of paper, draw your subject, like this astronaut, for example.

2. Put your acetate sheet on top of the drawing and start to color it, but remember to leave areas uncolored that you want to be blank.

Try to always paint in the same direction and with the point slightly at an angle. And remember, once the crayon is applied to the acetate it's really hard to erase!

3. Once you've finished the drawing, you can add papers to the underside of the sheet to create the effects you want, cutting or painting them to fit properly. In our example, we cut out the head of a boy from a photo and added it to the picture.

Still Life

Materials: crayons, pencil, drawing paper, acetate, piece of wood veneer, sandpaper, stylus or other pointy tool

By now you've learned lots of ways that you can use crayons to get different effects. Now it's time to put all that you've learned together! Use all the different techniques you know to paint a simple table setting.

A grouping of different objects together on a surface is called a **still life**. To paint each object, you will use a different crayon art technique.

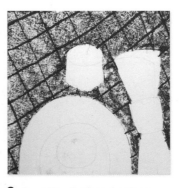

1. First make a sketch of all the objects you usually see on a table. In this example we've drawn a plate, water glass and napkin. Try to make your pencil lines light so they won't show under the crayon.

2. Next, trace the sketch you made and create a template of each object. Arrange the templates over the outlines of the objects in your sketch, and stick them down with tape. Then use the flat side of a crayon to fill in the texture of the tablecloth.

3. Draw the checkered pattern of the tablecloth using the tip of the crayon on top of the red background. You can take off the templates and you will see the reserves that you made on the paper.

4. On the napkin, paint dots with bright, warm tones, and smudge them with your fingers to blend them together.

5. Draw a thick border around the napkin edge in a color that goes well with the dots. Use a pointy tool to add small lines all the way around the edge to make it look like stitches.

6. On a very thin piece of wood veneer, draw the shape of the napkin ring and cut it out with scissors. Color it with lines or another pattern that you like.

7. Paint the water glass with watrcolor crayon in blue, and then, using a wet paintbrush, paint over the color until it has dissolved with the water.

8. When the water glass has dried, color over the glass with a white crayon for a see-through effect.

9. Now paint the tomato. If you remember how to create the effect of volume using complementary colors, figure out where to put the shadow on this red tomato using a green crayon. Paint a green stem as well.

10. Paint the plate in one color. Cut out the shape of a fork from a piece of sandpaper and color it, making sure that you can still see the sandpaper texture. Glue it on top of the table.

11. Cut out a piece of acetate in the shape of a tray. Color it, but without pressing too hard on the crayon so that it doesn't leave scratch lines. Then, with a pointy tool, you can make marks on it to make it look more like a tray. Glue it onto the tablecloth.

12. Have some fun and make it look like someone has dripped some ketchup on the table, and it has splattered on the tablecloth and the plate. You can make these drips by lighting a long taper candle and carefully letting the wax drip over your painting. Ask an adult to help you with this!

Have you noticed that this still life has been painted all in warm tones, except for the water and the stem of the tomato? Now you choose the tones you like the most and repeat this exercise to put in to practice everything you have learned. **Have fun!**